Blogging For Anyone

A Complete Guide to Success

by

David K. Ewen, M.Ed.

Part of the

"Professor Lecture Series"

Blogging for Anyone
A Complete Guide to Success
By David K. Ewen, M.Ed.

Published by Ewen Prime Company

Copyright © 2013, Ewen Prime Company

ISBN-13: **978-1483940434**
ISBN-10: **1483940438**

About the author

Professor David Ewen is an author, speaker, talk show host, film director, record producer, and publicist.   He founded Ewen Prime Company in 1994 by launching a publishing company. In 1998, Professor Ewen began his broadcasting and lecture tours.   Today he lectures on new digital media and publicity topics in the seven states of New York and New England.   Professor Ewen is also the founder of Forest Academy that houses content for his lectures.   He is also a consulting professor for the Saylor Foundation.

Other books by David K. Ewen, M.Ed.

Go to: http://davidewenpublished.webs.com/

Blogging For Anyone
A Complete Guide To Success

by

David K. Ewen, M.Ed.

www.ForestAcademy.org

Professor Lecture Series

David K. Ewen, M.Ed.
Forest Academy
www.ForestAcademy.org
ForestAcad@gmail.com
(413) 342-0418

www.ForestAcademy.org

Get and learn more at:

www.ForestAcademy.org

www.ForestAcademy.org

Prerequisite

The prerequisite to beginning blogging is to have some computer savviness. I've come across students who rarely use a computer and are to afraid to step onto the Internet. For those students, I recommend overall computer training in the following Microsoft suite of products

- Windows
- Explorer
- Office *

* The study of office can be limited to a brief overview of Microsoft Word.

Without this foundation, then the study of blogging would be far too advanced and confusing. This book assumes that a basic foundation exists. Before continuing further, determine if you have this prerequisite foundation.

Purpose

Blogging is a vehicle for sharing by writers. The trend of media is to have audience participation in the way of providing feedback and content as well as sharing your blog with others. This participation authenticates the quality of your content. If no one participates, then no one is interested. If that's true, then all you need is a pencil and paper to satisfy your writing.

Today's content in blogs is more than writing. People are living in a world of evolving multimedia technology. You need to be able to provide text, pictures, audio, and video content. Ask for feedback so that you can do more to provide satisfaction to your audience. An important feedback would help you determine how to get readers to come back on a regular basis. You want to have more than people stopping by once. Your audience grows if people come on a regular basis. You must have content that is tempting.

www.ForestAcademy.org

Genre

What do you want to write about? Who would be interested? What is the history of your topic? Are there news stories about your topic that you would like to follow up on? Go to http://news.google.com and search for news stories. Your audience interest would be a follow up on an actual news story.

Whatever it is you write about, it must be something that the audience can use. Not think about, but use. We live in a tangible world. People are looking for information that will help them. It may be career, hobby, relationship, or home life related. People are looking for something that goes beyond pondering. It must be something that has a positive influence on their own agenda, goals, hobby, faith, career, relationship, or home life.

For you genre and topic of interest, why did you choose it? How might others be influenced or benefit from your writing? What will you offer?

News Worthy

Are there news stories about your topic that you would like to follow up on? Go to **http://news. google.com** and search for news stories. A current news story already has an interest. Be hot on the story and be relevant.

Copyright

Beware that private intellectual property needing protecting from infringing on copyright protection must never be put online in a blog. Websites are worldwide and cannot be policed with international laws. Content that is needs this level of protection is more suited in the form of a book rather than a blog. See www.ForestAcademy.org for courses and books on book publishing.

Blogs are general sharing content that uses the participation of the audience comments to help build the content over time. Plan on your blog as a vehicle to solicit information with you as the author and subject matter expert.

Rated "G"

The internet is worldwide and accessible by nearly everyone. Exceptions include overseas government agency control. Certainly the United States is wide open.

Be conscious of what you are posting. Be aware of different age groups, ethnic groups, and belief groups. Plan on growing your audience in a friendly open public environment.

www.ForestAcademy.org

Tumbler is a digital media content sharing website.

Tumblr lets you effortlessly share anything.
Post text, photos, quotes, links, music, and videos from your browser, phone, desktop, email or wherever you happen to be. You can customize everything, from colors to your theme's HTML.

- Tumblr is a content sharing tool.
- You share written text, links, photos, videos
- Posting is done, online, email, mobile phone.

Wordpress

Wordpress.com is a blog site to share content with subscribers

People subscribe to follow just like a free magazine subscription

You can have stats to see who's following you and sharing your content

You can add pictures, videos, and audio

- Tips: **http://en.blog.wordpress.com/**
- Support: **http://en.support.wordpress.com/**

Facebook

A Facebook page or group is a collection of followers who can share in posts or you can restrict to you being the only author. Your page or group can be public or private. Facebook is by far the most popular social media site for sharing information. It is easy to share your written text, photos, and videos.

As you start your blog, your facebook friends are most likely your first subscribers. They will help build bring in other followers

Twitter

Whichever tool you use for Blog, you must also have Twitter as it is a short string (120 characters) content sharing tool. It is very common and popular similar to Facebook.

Hashtags "#" are hyperlinks to collect all twitter posts associated with having the same hashtag.

An example would be an event or location   #OurSpecialEventOnFriday.   It would have to be specific so that the hashtag is not duplicated by another person's efforts.

http://twitter.com   Your twitter feed is http://twitter.com/__your ID__

Twitter is a good way to share your blog and connect it to a hashtag that may have popularity. It helps build an audience and make new connections.

As with blogs, you can grow your followers on Twitter through facebook, email, and connecting through Hashtags.

www.ForestAcademy.org

The Google Advantage

Blogger.com from google

Create Google account. One account gives you access to the following

- Blog website as: http://__your ID__.BlogSpot.com
- YouTube channel to upload & share videos
- Phone # with voice mail at http://Voice.Google.com
- Email address with your ID being __your ID__@gmail.com
- Calendar of your events at http://Calendar.Google.com

Widgets for Blog

There are many widgets or tools that are used to help bring interest to your blog

Other widgets help your audience easily share your blog on Facebook and Twitter.

- http://www.widgetbox.com/tag/blogger

- http://www.way2blogging.org/

Meta Tags

Meta tags help make your blog or website searchable. Effectively placing meta tags means you have better SEO (search engine optimization).

Meta tags is HTML code that puts title and description of your blog or website behind the scenes and is not displayed. It is only used by the search engine for relevance.

This is a description meta tag that tells the search engine what your blog or website is about. Depending on what a person is looking for your site will show up on SERP (Search Engine Results Page)

<meta name="description" content="Awesome Description Here">

This line of code would be added using the HTML editor of your website or blog

Be Searchable

Increase your visibility by submitting and optimizing your website for Google search, and distributing your content across the web.

http://www.google.com/submityourcontent/website-owner

Also add your blog to Googe's blog search

http://blogsearch.google.com/ping

Add your blog to Yahoo and Bing search engines
http://www.bing.com/toolbox/submit-site-url
  (submitting to Bing will also submit to Yahoo)

www.ForestAcademy.org

Article Writing

Your blog can be in the form of an article that may include pictures and links to videos.   Write feature articles for Examiner, HubPages, and Demand Media Studios.

- www.Examiner.com
- www.HubPages.com
- www.demandstudios.com

You can receive a source of small revenue by people clicking ads on your article.   Writing for these sources is a freelance writers job. It is not considered a major source of income, but good quality content along with marketing and publicity can provide some revenue.

Blog Talk Radio

- Free outside of prime time (7p-11p)
- Free shows no longer than 30 minutes
- Suggest landline phone for call in
- Suggest cable internet for Studio Board
- Show is made available on iTunes
- www.BlogTalkRadio.com/_Show.Name.ID_
- Integrated automatically for Facebook updates

www.BlogTalkRadio.com

www.ForestAcademy.org

Cross Platform

Cross platform refers to mixing different types of media. For example you would have text content that would include a picture, embedded video, and a link to audio content. This would commonly be seen in your blog on blogger, Wordpress, and tumblr.

Your blog show on Blog Talk Radio has a written text section that could also include links to YouTube videos.

The description of your YouTube video can have links to your blog and radio show on Blog Talk Radio.

When you report on Examiner, HubPages, or Demand Studios, you can have links to your videos, radio shows, and blog.

Your blogging is spread out done in multiple locations

Marketing
&
Publicity

This training has repetitive redundancies to ensure easier, faster, comprehensive learning

www.ForestAcademy.org

Marketing and Publicity

Marketing and Publicity have two different meanings.   They are needed together. Each one cannot work successfully alone. The are effective together.

- <u>Marketing</u> are the elements that describe why your product is worth buying by the consumer

- <u>Publicity</u> is the vehicle to get the marketing elements to the consumer so they know about your product.

An example is a newspaper ad.

- What is written in the ad is the marketing
- The newspaper itself is the publicity

Both need to work together to be effective.   You need <u>marketing</u> and <u>publicity</u> together to reach the consumer to **explain why your product is worth buying**.

The following practice exercises will involve the example of an author and a book.

Three Elements of Marketing

Here are three elements of marketing that will in turn be distributed through publicity.

- <u>WIIFM</u> = What's In it For Me. A question to be answered; why the consumer should buy the product
- <u>RASCIL</u> factors represent the **Who** is the author & **What** is the book
- <u>5 W's</u> covers other elments and pulls WIIFM & RASCIL together

All three elements of marketing are combined.

Who

                 Who & What = RASCIL

What

When .... Time frame

Where .... Location

Why = WIIFM

Copyright (c) 2012, David K. Ewen, M.Ed.

www.ForestAcademy.org

Understanding WIIFM

WIIFM is What's In It For Me

WIIFM = (It/This) will (Make/Give) you __(why?/passion)__

Some examples are:

- It will make you happy
- This will make you successful
- It will give you chills
- This will give you love

WIIFM represents the

- Passion
- Why
- Result
- Impact

www.ForestAcademy.org

Understanding RASCIL

RASCIL defines the WHO and the WHAT of your product.

The WHO is about you the author ||| The WHAT is about your book

R = Reliability - how long have you been involved with your genre or topic
A = Authenticity - certifications, degrees, experience, positions, titles, participation
S = Simplicity to get your product
C = Completeness - All the satisfying qualities of your book
I = Illustration - Cover of your book
L = Location = Where the book can be purchased (stores, online, audio, ebook, paperback)

RASCIL

R & A represents the WHO in other words WHO is the author
S, C, I, L represents the WHAT about your book

```
R   WHO
A
-------------------------------------------------
S
C   WHAT
I
L
```

Marketing

This is the formula to represent yourself. It's easy to explain, but very hard to do.

- WIIFM = (It/This) will (Make/Give) you __(why?/passion)__
- RASCIL = Reliability, Authenticity, Simplicity, Completeness, Illustration, Location
- 5 W's = Who, What, When, Where, Why

Together, they have a combined formula / Copyright (c) 2012, David K. Ewen, M.Ed.

Who

What   Who & What = RASCIL

When .... Time frame

Where .... Location

Why = WIIFM

Copyright (c) 2012, David K. Ewen, M.Ed.

www.ForestAcademy.org

WIIFM is What's In It For Me

WIIFM = (It/This) will (Make/Give) you __(why?/passion)__

Some examples are:

- It will make you happy
- This will make you successful
- It will give you chills
- This will give you love

WIIFM represents the

- Passion
- Why
- Result
- Impact

RASCIL

Our next topic is on RASCIL.   First
we'll do a quick review of WIIFM
because that is a very difficult topic.   It's
easy to explain and understand, but
putting it into practice is difficult because
it does not follow the natural way of
thinking.

WIIFM Review

WIIFM = What's In It For Me

WIIFM is a question from your reader about your book
They are asking "What's In It For Me" (WIIFM)

Your answer to your reader about your book is your answer to WIIFM

Answer to WIIFM is (It/This) will (Make/Give) you _"emotion"_

There are four different ways to answer WIIFM

    (1) It will make you ___
    (2) This will make you ___
    (3) It will give you ___
    (4) This will give you ___

R.A.S.C.I.L.

RASCIL represent the WHO & WHAT. It is to be used as a general guide to help ensure facts aren't missed.

The origin of RASCIL is the design of yellow page ads

R = Reliability
A = Authenticity
S = Simplicity
C = Completeness
I = Illustration
L = Location

Use an example of a family owned auto mechanic garage in the yellow pages.

R = Reliability   ... Since 1976
A = Authenticity   ... ACE Certified
S = Simplicity   ... Early drop off, weekend hours
C = Completeness   ... oil change, mufflers, auto body repair, tires
I = illustration   ... Picture of clean garage with tools hanging neatly
L = Location   ... Address, phone

Understanding RASCIL

RASCIL defines the WHO and the WHAT of your product.

The WHO is about you the author ||| The WHAT is about your book

R = Reliability - how long have you been involved with your genre or topic
A = Authenticity - certifications, degrees, experience, positions, titles, participation
S = Simplicity to get your product
C = Completeness - All the satisfying qualities of your book
I = Illustration - Cover of your book
L = Location = Where the book can be purchased (stores, online, audio, ebook, paperback)

RASCIL

R & A represents the WHO in other words WHO is the author
S, C, I, L represents the WHAT about your book

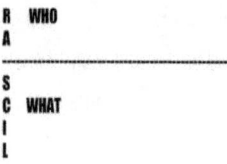

www.ForestAcademy.org

An example of RASCIL for an author. Let's pretend I am a cardiologist wrote a book about eating healthy called Delicious Success With Your Health. The doctor part isn't true, but the book is.

- R = Reliability
- A = Authenticity
- S = Simplicity
- C = Completeness
- I = Illustration
- L = Location

Delicious Success
With Your Health

POWER SALADS FOR
A POWERFUL YOU

DAVID K. EWEN, M.ED.

Example of RASCIL to describe Who & What

Definitions

- R = Reliability
- A = Authenticity
- S = Simplicity
- C = Completeness
- I = Illustration
- L = Location

Example

- R = Dr. David Ewen
- A = Doctor from ABC Hospital
- S = Easy to order online (Amazon, B&N)
- C = Different risks heart disease, diabetes, cancer
- I = Cover of the book
- L = Book found at Barnes and Noble & Amazon

The Five W's cover other elements in marketing. It also includes the WIIFM and the RASCIL factors. The 5 W's are (1) WHO (2) WHAT (3) WHEN (4) WHERE (5) WHY

The WHO and the WHAT are the RASCIL factors describing the content creator and the product.   For example the RASCIL factors describe the author and the book in identifying terms "who" and "what"

The WHY is the answer to WIIFM. This is the question the consumer is asking about your product

To understand the 5 W's, it is important to review WIIFM and RASCIL briefly.

- *The WHEN is any type of time frame represented - This is very flexible*

- *The WHERE is any type of location represented - This is also very flexible*

Next, we will do a quick review of WIIFM and RASCIL before pulling it all together.

WIIFM Review

WIIFM is a question from your reader about your book
They are asking "What's In It For Me" (WIIFM)

Your answer to your reader about your book is your answer to
WIIFM

Answer to WIIFM is (It/This) will (Make/Give) you _"emotion"_

There are four different ways to answer WIIFM

      (1) It will make you ___
      (2) This will make you ___
      (3) It will give you ___
      (4) This will give you ___

RASCIL review

RASCIL defines the WHO and the WHAT of your product.

The **WHO** is about you the author ||| The **WHAT** is about your book

R = <u>Reliability</u> - how long have you been involved with your genre or topic

A = <u>Authenticity</u> - certifications, degrees, experience, positions, titles, participation

S = <u>Simplicity</u> - easy to get your product

C = <u>Completeness</u> - all the satisfying qualities of your book

I = <u>Illustration</u> - cover of your book

L = <u>Location</u> = where the book can be purchased (stores, online, audio, ebook, paperback)

<u>RASCIL</u>

- R & A represents the WHO in other words WHO is the author
- S. C, I, L represents the WHAT about your book

Pulling It All Together

This is the formula to represent yourself. It's easy to explain, but very hard to do.

- WIIFM = (It/This) will (Make/Give) you __(why?/passion)__
- RASCIL = Reliability, Authenticity, Simplicity, Completeness, Illustration, Location
- 5 W's = Who, What, When, Where, Why

Together, they have a combined formula / Copyright (c) 2012, David K. Ewen, M.Ed.

Who

What   Who & What = RASCIL

When .... Time frame

Where .... Location

Why = WIIFM

Copyright (c) 2012, David K. Ewen, M.Ed.

I'll talk about the same book twice.

Example

- WHO   Dr. David Ewen
- WHAT   Wrote a book about eating healthy
- WHEN   There will be a book signing next week
- WHERE   Signing at Barnes & Noble
- WHY   It will make you feel great

Same book, but described in another way

- WHO   Award winning cardiologist
- WHAT   The need to eat healthy
- WHEN   It's never too late
- WHERE   All across America
- WHY   This will give you good health

Remember the

- WHEN is any type of Time Frame
- WHERE is any type of Location

Delicious Success
With Your Health
POWER SALADS FOR
A POWERFUL YOU

DAVID K. EWEN, M.Ed.

www.ForestAcademy.org

Practice Your Publicity

Find on Amazon.com

Publicity Made Simple: Success With Media Relations

www.ForestAcademy.org

Congratulations You Are Ready To Start Blogging

www.ForestAcademy.org

Get and learn more at:

www.ForestAcademy.org

Blogging For Anyone
A Complete Guide To Success

by

David K. Ewen, M.Ed.

www.ForestAcademy.org

www.ingramcontent.com/pod-product-compliance
Lightning Source LLC
Chambersburg PA
CBHW051225170526
45166CB00005B/2043